DAK PRESCOTT

BY ALLAN MOREY

BELLWETHER MEDIA · MINNEAPOLIS, MN

TORQUE

Torque brims with excitement perfect for thrill-seekers of all kinds. Discover daring survival skills, explore uncharted worlds, and marvel at mighty engines and extreme sports. In *Torque* books, anything can happen. Are you ready?

This edition first published in 2023 by Bellwether Media, Inc.

No part of this publication may be reproduced in whole or in part without written permission of the publisher. For information regarding permission, write to Bellwether Media, Inc., Attention: Permissions Department, 6012 Blue Circle Drive, Minnetonka, MN 55343.

Library of Congress Cataloging-in-Publication Data

LC record for Dak Prescott available at: https://lccn.loc.gov/2022050042

Editor: Rebecca Sabelko   Designer: Josh Brink

Printed in the United States of America, North Mankato, MN.

TABLE OF CONTENTS

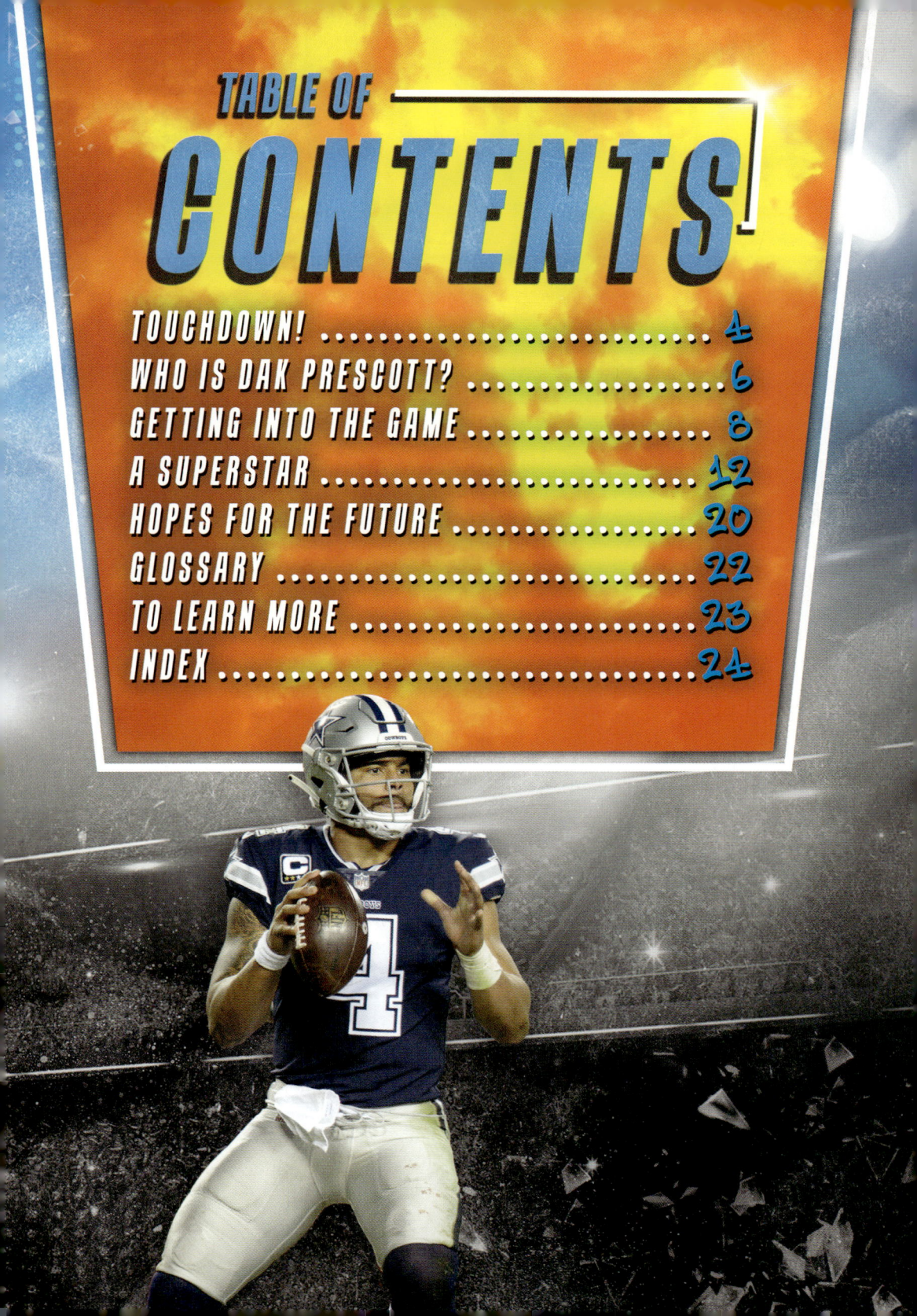

TOUCHDOWN!

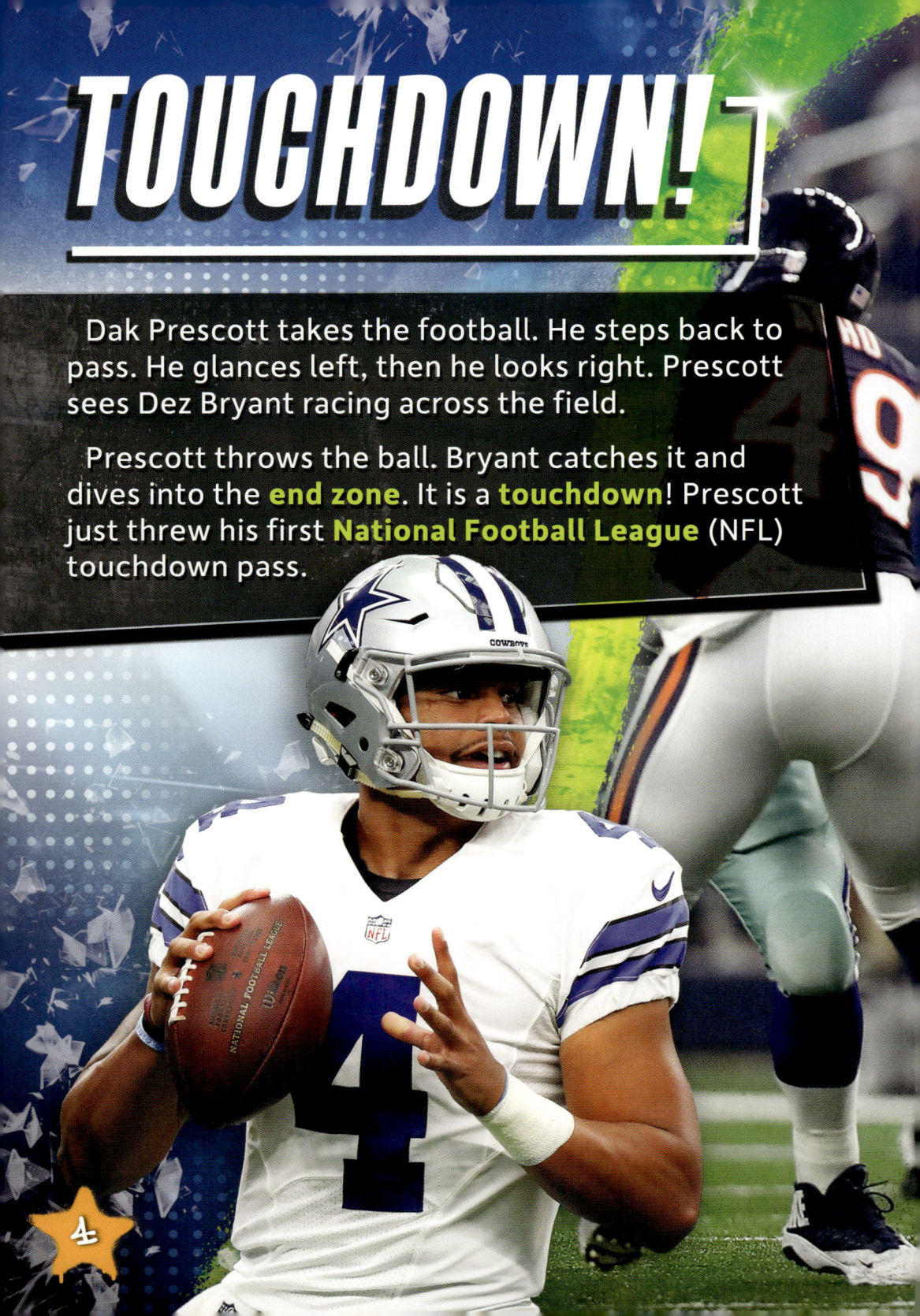

Dak Prescott takes the football. He steps back to pass. He glances left, then he looks right. Prescott sees Dez Bryant racing across the field.

Prescott throws the ball. Bryant catches it and dives into the **end zone**. It is a **touchdown**! Prescott just threw his first **National Football League** (NFL) touchdown pass.

WHO IS DAK PRESCOTT?

Dak Prescott is the **quarterback** for the Dallas Cowboys. He has been the leader of the team since the beginning of the 2016 season.

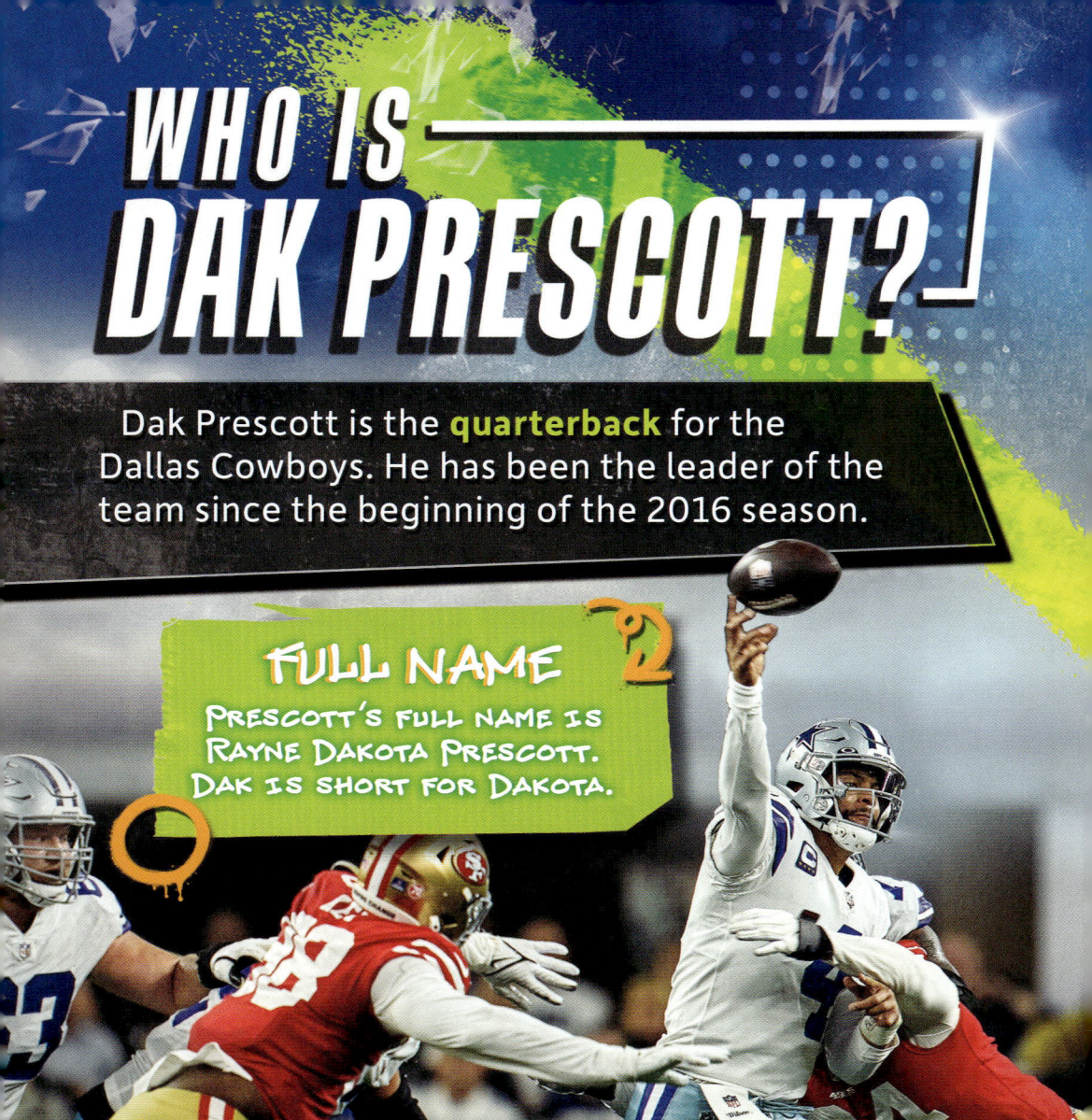

FULL NAME

PRESCOTT'S FULL NAME IS RAYNE DAKOTA PRESCOTT. DAK IS SHORT FOR DAKOTA.

6

DAK PRESCOTT

BIRTHDAY	July 29, 1993
HOMETOWN	Sulphur, Louisiana
POSITION	quarterback
HEIGHT	6 feet 2 inches
DRAFTED	Dallas Cowboys in the 4th round (135th overall) of the 2016 NFL Draft

Prescott has a strong throwing arm. In his **career**, he has thrown for more than 140 touchdowns. He is also quick on his feet. He has run for more than 20 touchdowns.

GETTING INTO THE GAME

Prescott began playing football in his backyard with his older brothers. In youth football, he played different positions. But he became a quarterback in middle school.

PRESCOTT COACHING AT HAUGHTON HIGH SCHOOL

8

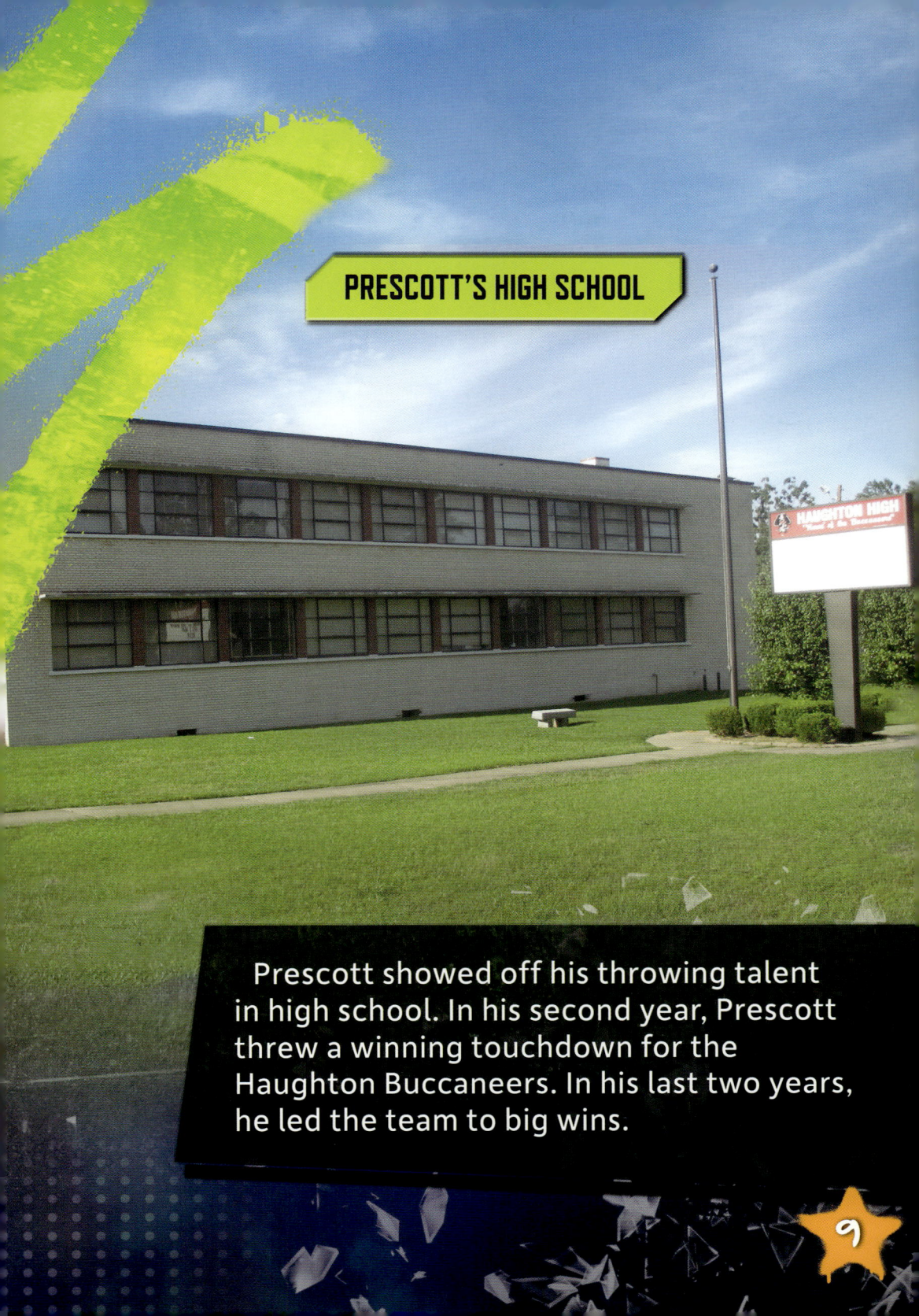

PRESCOTT'S HIGH SCHOOL

Prescott showed off his throwing talent in high school. In his second year, Prescott threw a winning touchdown for the Haughton Buccaneers. In his last two years, he led the team to big wins.

In 2011, Prescott joined the Mississippi State Bulldogs. He became their starting quarterback in 2013. That year, he led the Bulldogs to win the **Liberty Bowl**.

As a Bulldog, he threw 29 touchdown passes throughout the 2015 season. He also threw for 3,793 yards. He was ready for the NFL!

PRESCOTT IN THE LIBERTY BOWL

KEEPING MOM CLOSE

PRESCOTT'S MOM PASSED AWAY IN 2013. SHE WAS HIS BIGGEST FAN. SHE HELPED HIM STICK WITH FOOTBALL. HE KEEPS HER CLOSE WITH A "MOM" TATTOO ON HIS WRIST.

FAVORITES

HOBBY	FOOD	COLOR	MOVIE
fishing	fried boudin	gray	Remember the Titans

11

A SUPERSTAR

During the 2016 NFL **Draft**, few teams were interested in Prescott. Most thought he would be a backup quarterback.

PRESCOTT'S TRAINING

12

TONY ROMO

But the Dallas Cowboys took a chance on him. They picked Prescott in the fourth round. He began the season as a backup to Tony Romo. Romo had led the team for the past 10 seasons.

13

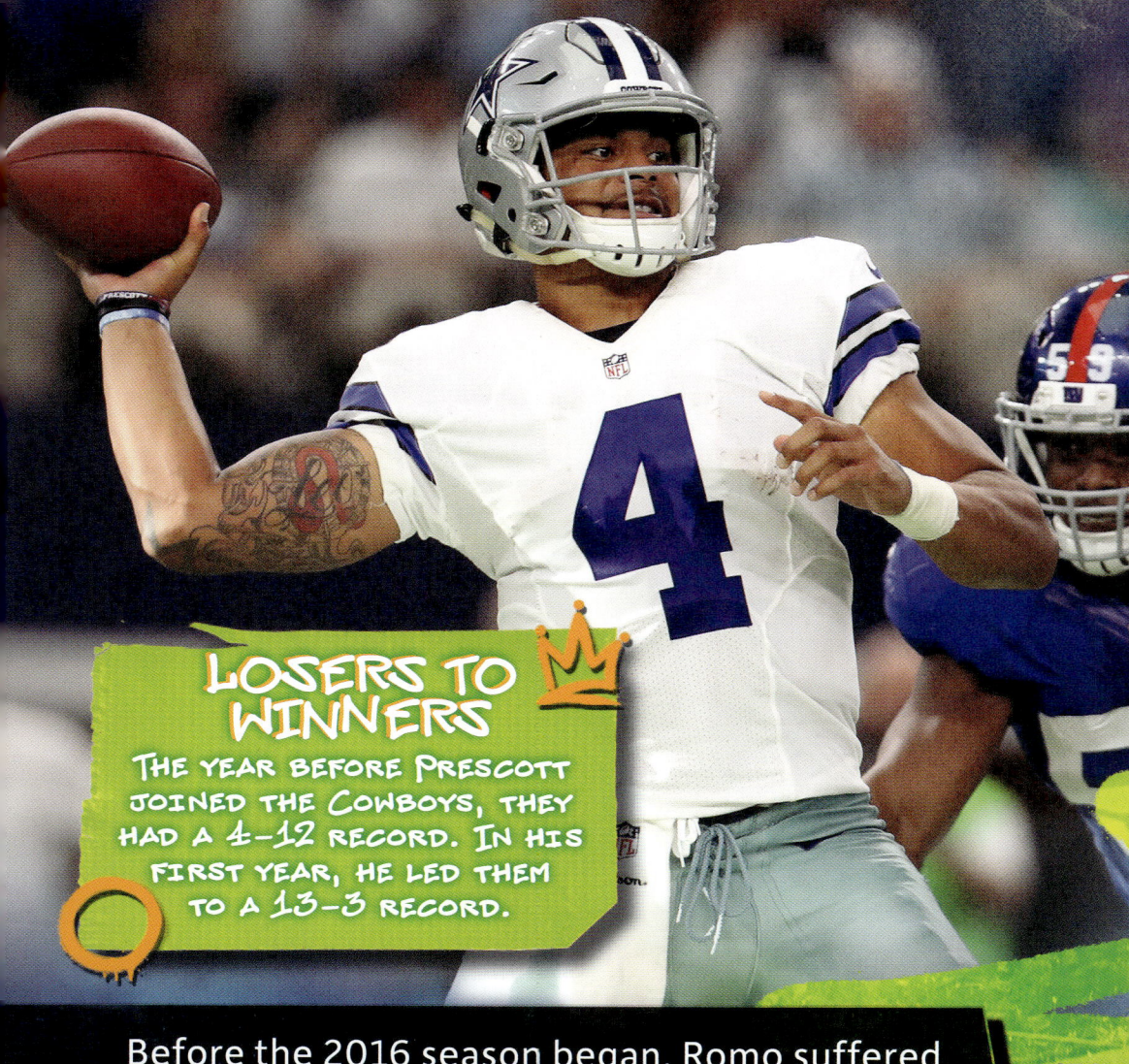

LOSERS TO WINNERS

THE YEAR BEFORE PRESCOTT JOINED THE COWBOYS, THEY HAD A 4–12 RECORD. IN HIS FIRST YEAR, HE LED THEM TO A 13–3 RECORD.

Before the 2016 season began, Romo suffered an injury. Prescott became the starter during the first game of the season.

During his **rookie** year, Prescott proved he was a star in the NFL. He led the Cowboys to the **playoffs**. He was also voted the NFL's **Offensive** Rookie of the Year.

14

DAK PRESCOTT MAP

◉ **Dallas Cowboys, Dallas, Texas** **2016** to present

2016 NFL OFFENSIVE ROOKIE OF THE YEAR

15

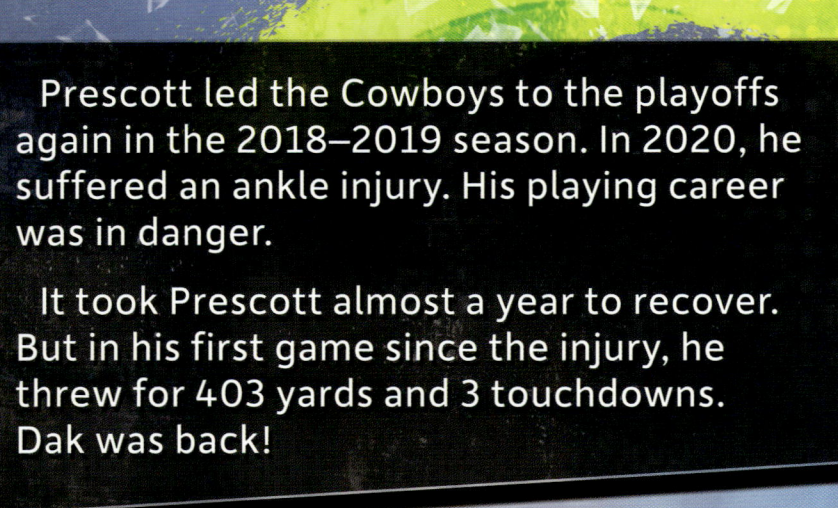

Prescott led the Cowboys to the playoffs again in the 2018–2019 season. In 2020, he suffered an ankle injury. His playing career was in danger.

It took Prescott almost a year to recover. But in his first game since the injury, he threw for 403 yards and 3 touchdowns. Dak was back!

TROPHY SHELF

Liberty Bowl MVP

NFL Offensive Rookie of the Year

Senior Bowl Most Outstanding Player

Prescott had one of the best years of his career in 2021. He threw a team-record 37 touchdown passes. He also led the Cowboys back to the playoffs. But he struggled to play well in the playoffs.

Prescott's 2022 season got off to a rough start. He injured his hand during the first game. But he worked hard to get back on the field.

TIMELINE

— 2011 —

Prescott joins the Mississippi State Bulldogs football team

— 2013 —

Prescott and the Bulldogs win the Liberty Bowl

18

— 2016 —

Prescott is drafted by the Cowboys and becomes the starting quarterback

— 2017 —

Prescott wins NFL Offensive Rookie of the Year

HOPES FOR THE FUTURE

Prescott is set to be the Cowboys' starting quarterback for the coming seasons. He hopes to lead them to the playoffs and win a **Super Bowl**.

He will also continue helping others. Prescott founded the Faith Fight Finish **Foundation** to help families in need. While his throwing arm makes him a football star, his work to help others makes him a hero!

21

GLOSSARY

career—the job that a person has for most of their professional life

draft—a process during which professional teams choose high school and college players to play for them

end zone—the area on either end of a football field

foundation—an organization that helps people and communities

Liberty Bowl—a post-season college football game played by major college football teams

National Football League—a professional football league in the United States; the National Football League is often called the NFL.

offensive—related to players who have the ball and are trying to score

playoffs—games played after the regular season is over; playoff games determine which teams play in the Super Bowl.

quarterback—a player on offense whose main job is to throw and hand off the ball

rookie—related to a first-year player in a sports league

Super Bowl—the annual championship game of the National Football League

touchdown—a score that occurs when a team crosses into their opponent's end zone with the football; a touchdown is worth six points.

22

TO LEARN MORE

AT THE LIBRARY

Fishman, Jon M. *Dak Prescott*. Minneapolis, Minn.: Lerner Publications, 2019.

Goodman, Michael E. *Dallas Cowboys*. Mankato, Minn.: Creative Education, 2023.

Storm, Marysa. *Highlights of the Dallas Cowboys*. Mankato, Minn.: Black Rabbit Books, 2019.

ON THE WEB

FACTSURFER

Factsurfer.com gives you a safe, fun way to find more information.

1. Go to www.factsurfer.com

2. Enter "Dak Prescott" into the search box and click 🔍.

3. Select your book cover to see a list of related content.

INDEX